Writing

Glossary

Answers

Speaking and listening skills

Planning to talk

Speaking in front of a group can be daunting. Being well prepared for your presentation will calm your nerves and ensure that you speak effectively.

Gather the information you need. Use books, the Internet, TV and radio programmes to find interesting information. Make a note of all your ideas, pick out the most important ones and decide which order to put them in.

Next, spend some time thinking about how to present your ideas. Reading out a whole presentation like a script won't sound very natural. Instead, jot down bullet points to remind you of the key points as you speak. It will sound much better and engage your audience.

Listening

Listening quietly while other people talk isn't just being polite. It will enable you to listen really carefully to what they say. Taking notes will remind you of a speaker's key points, so you can respond to them when it is your turn to speak. Jot down anything you disagree with, or anything you would like to ask a question about.

Questions

Asking questions is a great way to find out more information. Being able to ask sensible questions after someone has been speaking shows that you have been listening carefully. You could ask for more information, or find out how the speaker feels about the topic.

When you are preparing to speak, think about the questions people might ask you, so you have good answers ready.

Success
Learn and Practise

English
age 10-11 · level four

YEAR

6

Alison Head

Contents

Planning to talk

Imagine you have been asked to do a presentation on an endangered animal of your choice. Do some research to find out where it lives, how many are left and what is being done to protect them. Write down three pieces of information you could use as a prompt.

1 _____

2 _____

3 _____

`3`

Listening

Working in pairs, have a discussion about whether you think wearing school uniform is a good idea. Listen carefully to what your partner says.

1 Write down one point you agree with.

_____

_____

2 Write down one point you disagree with.

_____

_____

`2`

Questions

Write down a question you could ask to find out more about your partner's opinion.

_____

_____

`1`

TOTAL MARKS `6`

The language of books

The features of books

Back covers often carry a blurb, which is designed to give a taster of what is inside the book. Back covers also carry the ISBN, a unique number which helps libraries and bookshops identify the book.

Inside, books often contain contents lists at the front and indexes at the back. The contents page lists the chapters or sections and what page each one starts on. The alphabetical index shows where each topic appears in the book.

Books that contain difficult new words may also have a glossary at the back, which explains what they mean.

Top Tip *Turn to the back of this book to see what a glossary looks like.*

Using the features of books

The features of books are there to make reading them easier. Look at how the information could help you.

"I need to find out about lions."	Look under l in the index.
"I have to read chapter 6 for homework."	Find out what page it begins on by looking at the contents list.
"I need to order a new book at the library."	Use the ISBN.
"I've found a new word I don't know."	Look in the glossary for the definition.
"I can't find a book I want to read."	Read the blurb on different books, until you find one that interests you.

 Key words   blurb   ISBN   index   glossary

The features of books

Think about your favourite book, or the book you are reading at the moment. Write a short blurb for the back cover to attract readers.

_____

_____

_____

_____

_____

_____

_____

Top Tip *Blurbs give a clue as to what a story is about, but they often leave a question hanging too, e.g. Will Daniel find the key in time?*

1

Using the features of books

Write a sentence to explain how each of these features could help you to read a book.

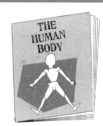

1 The blurb

_____

2 The ISBN

_____

3 The contents list

_____

4 The glossary

_____

4

TOTAL MARKS   5

Fiction and non-fiction

Features of fiction

Fiction is made-up writing from the imagination of the writer. Short stories and novels are both fictional, even though they may be based on a real person, or on events that really took place. Fiction tells a story, so you need to read it all the way through to find out what happens. If you read the chapters in the wrong order, you would lose the thread of the story!

Good fiction writing flows well and is fast-paced, so that you can read quickly to find out what happens next. The best fiction is so gripping that you cannot put it down until it is finished!

Stories for young children often have colourful pictures, but fiction for older children and adults tends not to be illustrated. Instead, writers use really descriptive language to help their readers imagine how things look.

Features of non-fiction

Non-fiction is information writing. There are lots of different types, including information books, newspapers, adverts and instructions.

Non-fiction books contain lots of facts, organised into chapters or sections, so that readers can find the information they need without reading the whole book.

Information writing often has lots of illustrations, like pictures, tables and diagrams. They help to make the writing easier to understand. The authors of non-fiction often choose impersonal language that helps to explain and describe things.

 Key words   fiction   non-fiction

Features of fiction

Find a fiction book you have not read before. Read the first page, then answer these questions.

1   Did the first page grab your attention and make you want to read on? Explain why.

   _____

   _____

2   Does the book contain pictures?

   _____

3   Does the author use description to help you to imagine the characters and setting?

   _____

   _____

3

Features of non-fiction

Circle the features you might find in a non-fiction book.

description of
characters

charts and diagrams

lots of facts

information
organised to make
facts easy to find

a storyline that runs
through the book

3

TOTAL MARKS   6

Reading skills

Skimming and scanning

Skimming is reading quickly right through a text to find out what it is about. Look for whether it is fiction or non-fiction and what kind of text it is. Also look out for special features, like sub-headings and bullet points.

Scanning means sweeping through a text to find key words to help you answer a question. The wording of the question will tell you what kind of information you need to find.

Where?	Look for a place name.
Who?	Look for the name of a person.
When?	Look for a date or time.
Why?	Look for the reason that something happened.

London >

Top Tip

Often, the wording of a question will mirror words in the text, e.g. **Mum hunted high and low for her keys,** *because she was late for work. Why did* **Mum hunt high and low for her keys?**

Deciding what you think

Some questions in reading comprehension tests will ask for your opinion about something in the text. You need to decide what you think, then find evidence in the text to back up your idea.

Q: Do you think the writer feels that recycling is a good idea?

A: I think the writer does feel that recycling is a good idea, because he says that recycling protects the environment by preventing waste from being buried in landfill sites.

Remember, you will get more marks if you can use evidence from the text to say why you have an opinion.

Key words   skimming   scanning   comprehension   opinion

Skimming and scanning

Write down whether you would use skimming or scanning to find each piece of information.

1 Whether a text is fiction or non-fiction. _____

2 The date of the Great Fire of London. _____

3 The location of Stonehenge. _____

4 What a short story is about. _____

5 How the writer has set out the information. _____

5

Deciding what you think

Read the text, then answer the questions.

Forward-thinking Cranville School installed its wind turbine last year and, along with its solar panels, is now able to heat its outdoor pool and provide renewable power to classrooms. The turbine saves school funds and provides renewable energy. Surely it would make sense for other schools to install their own wind turbines and solar panels in the future.

1 Do you feel that the writer thinks that Cranville School's wind turbine is a good idea? Why?

_____

_____

2 Do you think the writer feels that other schools should do the same?

_____

3 Do you think your school should install a wind turbine? Why?

_____

Top Tip *If a question about a text asks for your opinion, always back it up with evidence from the text.*

3

TOTAL MARKS **8**

Authors and narrators

What is a narrator?

The person who writes a text is called the author. Fiction authors use their imagination to create made-up stories, but that doesn't mean the story is always told using their voice.

The storyteller in a piece of fiction is called the narrator and the story is told from their viewpoint. Sometimes, the narrator is the author.

> The family scrambled through the ticket barrier and made a dash for the train.

In this sentence, the narrator is describing the action, without actually being involved in it.

At other times, the narrator is a character in the story.

> I pushed the children through the ticket barrier and we made a dash for the train.

Do you see that the story is being told in the voice of one of the characters?

Narrator and viewpoint

Who the narrator is will affect how the story works and how the reader reacts to it.

Narrators who are not part of the story can tell the reader things that none of the characters know. This can help to build suspense because the reader wants to know how the characters will react as events unfold.

Narrators who are part of the story may not be able to tell the reader how the other characters are feeling. However, the reader will want to get to know the character who is narrating and will be keen to find out what happens to them in the end.

Top Tip *It is possible for stories to have more than one narrator, with parts of the story told from the viewpoint of different characters.*

 Key words   author   narrator   viewpoint

What is a narrator?

Read these sentences and decide whether the narrator is a character in the story or not. Write a sentence to explain your answer.

1   The school bell rang as Max crossed the lane at the bottom of the hill. He was going to be late again!

_____

_____

2   Auntie Jane produced my bridesmaid's dress with a flourish and I gasped in horror at the lime green frills.

_____

_____

2

Narrator and viewpoint

1   Explain why an author might choose a narrator who is not part of the story.

_____

_____

_____

_____

2   How might the reader feel about a narrator who is also a character in the story?

_____

_____

_____

_____

2

TOTAL MARKS   4

Life stories

Biography

A **biography** is the life story of a person that is written by someone else. Biographies are written in the **third person**. That means that the author is writing about the life of someone else and focuses on what he or she does.

> **His** football career began at Chelsea, where **he** scored 15 goals in **his** first season.

> **She** left school at 18 and trained as a secretary. A local film production company offered **her** a job and it was here that **she** met **her** future husband.

Biography is non-fiction and writers research their subjects carefully to get the facts right.

Top Tip *It can sometimes be hard to tell whether what you are reading is fiction or fact, because most fiction tells the story of a character's life.*

Autobiography

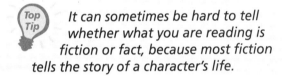

Autobiographies are life stories too. They are written by the person whose story they tell, so they are written in the **first person**. That means that the words show that the writer is telling his or her own story.

> **My** football career began at Chelsea, where **I** scored 15 goals in **my** first season.

> **I** left school at 18 and trained as a secretary. A local film production company offered **me** a job and it was here that **I** met **my** future husband.

Autobiography is non-fiction, but the writer's opinion will affect the way it is written. The author decides which events they tell the reader about and how to describe things.

 Key words   biography   third person   autobiography   first person

Biography

Think of someone you admire. Write down five things you would need to find out about if you were going to write their biography.

1 _____

2 _____

3 _____

4 _____

5 _____

○ 5

Autobiography

Answer these questions about autobiography.

1 What is autobiography? Write your own definition.

_____

2 Underline the sentence that comes from an autobiography. Write a sentence to explain your answer.

He raised an army and marched north to York.

We travelled to Paris to meet our parents.

_____

3 Write a sentence to explain why you think people might be interested in reading an autobiography.

_____

_____

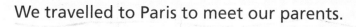

Top Tip *Remember, autobiography will contain words like **I, me, we, my, our**.*

○ 3

TOTAL MARKS ○ 8

15

Sentences

LEARN

WRITING

Simple sentences

Sentences are groups of words that work together to make sense on their own. Sentences are made up of clauses. A clause is a smaller group of words that contains a verb and a subject. A subject is the person or thing doing the action.

Simple sentences contain one clause.

The girl ran home.

subject   verb

Too many simple sentences make reading hard work, because the reader will pause at each full stop.

Top Tip

Compound sentences

Compound sentences contain two clauses that are equally important to the meaning of the sentence. In a compound sentence, each clause would make sense on its own and they are joined by a special word called a conjunction.

Sam kicked the ball and it broke the window.

clause 1   conjunction   clause 2

Complex sentences

A complex sentence has one main clause and one or more less important clauses that are called subordinate clauses. The main clause would make sense on its own, but the subordinate clauses would not.

Tom ran off to play football, although it was raining.

main clause   subordinate clause

Key words | sentence   clause   verb   subject   simple sentence
compound sentence   conjunction   complex sentence
main clause   subordinate clause

Simple and compound sentences

Write down the two simple sentences that have been joined to make each of these compound sentences.

1 Kate had a cold drink because she was thirsty.

K

_____

_____

2 Max found his key and he unlocked the door.

_____

_____

3 Jenny loves pasta but Tim likes pizza.

_____

_____

6

Complex sentences

Underline the main clause in these complex sentences.

1 Mum pegged the washing on the line, so it would dry.

2 Amy worked hard, tidying her bedroom.

3 Katie ran through the rain, dodging the puddles as she went.

4 We left for school early, so we wouldn't be late.

4

TOTAL MARKS 10

Contractions

What are contractions?

Often when we use two words together a lot, we end up joining them together. This is called contraction. One or more letters are taken out and replaced with an apostrophe to make the new word.

I would = I'd

we are = we're

it is = it's

they will = they'll

did not = didn't

she is = she's

they will = they'll

I am = I'm

who is = who's

is not = isn't

Using contracted forms

We join words together all the time when we are speaking, and contractions are useful when you are writing dialogue for characters in your stories.

"**We're** off to the cinema!" said Sam.

You can also use them when you are writing informal letters or emails to your friends.

Dear Dawn, **I've** got some great news!

You would not usually use them in more formal writing, like school work or formal letters.

Red squirrels **have not** been seen in this area for many years.

Top Tip *In a writing test, think carefully about the type of writing you have been asked to write. You could lose marks if you use contractions in formal writing.*

 Key words   contraction   apostrophe   dialogue

What are contractions?

Write these sentences again, replacing each green word pair with the correct contracted form.

1 My uncle is great because he is a footballer.

_____

2 Mum says she will ring to find out what time to collect us.

_____

3 "You are the winner!" announced the judge.

_____

4 Katie yawned, "I am exhausted!"

_____

4

Using contracted forms

Think about each type of writing and decide whether you would use contractions in it. Write yes or no in the box.

1 An email to a pen pal.

2 A history report.

3 A letter to a local business, asking them to donate a raffle prize.

4 A piece of dialogue for a character in a story.

5 Direct speech to go in a speech bubble on a cartoon strip you are drawing.

6 A swimming certificate.

6

TOTAL MARKS 10

Possessive apostrophes

Using possessive apostrophes

Possessive apostrophes can be used to say that something belongs to someone or something.

When you are talking about just one person or thing, you add an apostrophe then *s*.

the cap that belongs to Claire = Claire's cap

If the word already ends in *s* because it is a plural, you just put an apostrophe at the end, without adding another *s*.

the trainers that belong to the boys = the boys' trainers

> **Top Tip**
> Some *singular* words end in *s*. Sometimes you just add an apostrophe, e.g. Giles' house. Other times you add an apostrophe then **s**, e.g. Thomas's book.

Its and it's

It is easy to get mixed up between *its* and *it's*. You need to remember that *its* does not have an apostrophe when you are saying that something belongs to *it*.

The bird spread **its** wings.

It's is the contracted form of *it is*.

It's cold today.

Key words   possessive apostrophe   plural   singular

Using possessive apostrophes

Add the possessive apostrophes to these sentences.

1 Our puppys toys are in its basket.

2 The twins desks are side by side.

3 The suns rays shone through the window.

4 Two ponies saddles hung on the wall.

5 Jacobs dad is a fireman.

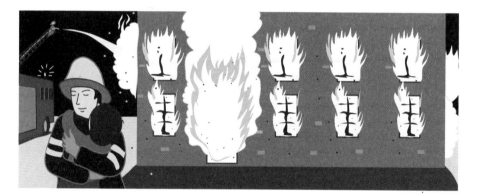

5

Its and it's

Choose *its* or *it's* to complete each sentence.

1 The gate squeaks when _____ opened.

2 The dog chased _____ tail.

3 Mum put the key back on _____ hook.

4 _____ too cold to swim in the sea.

5 The horse shook _____ mane.

5

TOTAL MARKS   10

Punctuation

Commas

Punctuation marks help to make your writing clearer, showing readers when they need to pause, when someone is speaking and when a sentence has finished.

Commas are particularly useful, as they help to make your writing easier to understand. They show readers when they need to pause and help to separate the different parts of a sentence.

   As time went on, Billy began to forget his old friends.

Commas can also be used to separate items in lists.

   I invited Claire, Sarah, Megan and Lucy to my party.

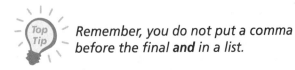 *Remember, you do not put a comma before the final **and** in a list.*

Colons and semi-colons

Colons and semi-colons can both be used to separate parts of sentences.

Semi-colons can join two clauses in a sentence, where one clause adds information to the other. Often they join two simple sentences.

   The dog shook himself. He had been caught in the rain.

   The dog shook himself; he had been caught in the rain.

Semi-colons can also be used to separate items in a list, especially when the items are more than one word long.

Colons can be used to introduce explanations or lists.

   You will need: scissors, glue, tissue paper and white card.

 Key words   comma   colon   semi-colon

Commas

Add the missing commas to these sentences.

1 When we got hungry we ate our picnic.

2 Last summer we went to Spain.

3 Billy went to bed yawning loudly.

4 Eventually the sun came out.

5 The dog ran after the postman barking as he went.

5

Colons and semi-colons

Write these pairs of sentences again as one sentence, by joining them with a semi-colon.

1 We took a picnic. It was a lovely day.

_____

2 I love Chinese food. Max prefers Italian meals.

_____

3 I found my umbrella. It was starting to rain.

_____

4 The sea was rough. We could not swim.

_____

5 The doorbell rang. My friends had arrived.

_____

5

TOTAL MARKS   10

Writing about speech

Direct and reported speech

There are two ways writers can write about what people say.

Direct speech uses the actual words that someone says. Speech punctuation shows that someone is talking and separates their words from the rest of the sentence.

Speech marks go at the beginning and the end of what the person says.

> Noticing the broken vase, Mum asked, "However did that happen?"

Reported speech is where the writer tells the reader about what someone has said, without using their actual words. Reported speech does not need speech marks.

> Mum asked us how the vase had been broken.

Introducing direct speech

When you write dialogue for your characters, it is important to tell your reader who is speaking, so that they can keep track of the conversation. You can do this before or after the speech.

> "Hello," called **Joe**.
>
> **Serena** replied, "Hi!"

Try to avoid using the verb *said* when you are introducing speech. Think of better alternatives that give the reader information about how the character is talking and whether what they are saying is a question or a command.

> "It's mine!" **insisted** Carl.
>
> "No it isn't!" **argued** Paul.

Top Tip: Try to use a variety of direct and reported speech when you are writing a story.

 Key words   direct speech   speech marks   reported speech

Direct and reported speech

Write these sentences of reported speech again, using direct speech.

1   The bus driver explained that there were empty seats at the back.

_____

2   Mrs Drew told us to get ready for assembly.

_____

3   Ben asked if he could have a strawberry milkshake.

_____

4   Daisy whispered that the present was hidden under her bed.

_____

5   Ryan apologised for spilling his drink.

_____

5

Introducing direct speech

Choose a word from the box to complete each sentence.

cheered   comforted   reminded   insisted   asked

1   "Don't worry, we can mend it," _____ Mum.

2   "You must clean up your room," _____ Dad.

3   "Don't forget your homework," _____ the teacher.

4   "When is your birthday?" _____ Beth.

5   "Hurray!" _____ the class.

5

TOTAL MARKS   10

Nouns and pronouns

Common nouns

Nouns name things and common nouns name ordinary things.

 cloud

 mouse

 tomato

Proper nouns

Proper nouns name people, places and things like the days of the week and the months of the year.

 December

 India

 Grace

Proper nouns always begin with a capital letter, whether or not they appear at the start of a sentence.

Pronouns

Pronouns can sometimes replace nouns in a sentence to save you from using the same noun again and again.

The dog wagged its tail, so I gave **the dog** a biscuit.

The dog wagged its tail, so I gave **it** a biscuit.

Top Tip *All sentences contain at least one noun or pronoun.*

Different pronouns replace different nouns:

- *I*, *me* to talk about yourself
- *he*, *him* to talk about males
- *she*, *her* to talk about females
- *they*, *them* to talk about a group

- *we*, *us* to talk about yourself in a group
- *it* to talk about an object or animal.

 Key words   noun   common noun   proper noun   pronoun

Common nouns

Think of a sensible common noun to complete each sentence.

1   We went to see a film at the _____.

2   Dad parked the _____ outside the house.

3   I am reading a _____ about space exploration.

3

Proper nouns

Underline the proper nouns in each sentence that should start with a capital letter.

1   Last <u>wednesday</u> was christopher's birthday.

2   We are going to france on holiday this <u>august</u>.

3   The nile flows through <u>egypt</u>.

3

Pronouns

Underline the best pronoun from the brackets to complete each sentence.

1   We hid from my brother so he wouldn't see [them   him   <u>us</u>].

2   The wind rocked the tree until [he   she   <u>it</u>] was blown over.

3   Ben's shoes were dirty, so [<u>he</u>   her   they] cleaned [us   <u>them</u>   she].

4   Debbie's hamster escaped but [he   <u>she</u>   us] caught [she   them   <u>it</u>].

4

TOTAL MARKS   10

Plurals

Simple plurals

If there are two or more of a particular noun, this is called a plural. Most plurals are simple to spell. Many plural nouns end in *s*.

coat ➜ coats   door ➜ doors   friend ➜ friends

Singular nouns that end in *ss*, *x*, *z*, *ch* or *sh* end in *es* in the plural.

hiss ➜ hisses   tax ➜ taxes

witch ➜ witches   bush ➜ bushes

Words ending in *y*

For nouns that end in a vowel then *y*, you just add *s* to make the plural.

donkey ➜ donkeys

If the noun ends in a consonant then *y*, you must take off the *y* and add *ies* to make the plural.

baby ➜ babies

Words ending in *f*

If a noun ends in *f*, you usually have to change the *f* to *ves* instead.

leaf ➜ leaves

There are a few exceptions, including *roofs*.

Top Tip

*Words ending in **ff** just end in **s** in the plural, e.g. cliffs.*

Key words   vowel   consonant

Simple plurals

Choose *s* or *es* to turn these nouns into plurals.

1 fox _____

2 dish _____

3 plant _____

4 boss _____

5 watch _____

 Top Tip *Try saying plurals out loud. You can often hear the e sound in es plurals.*

5

Words ending in *y*

Write down the plural for these words.

1 key _____

2 puppy _____

3 play _____

4 fairy _____

4

Words ending in *f*

In your own words, write the spelling rule for the plurals of nouns ending in *f*. Remember to include any exceptions to the rule.

_____

_____

_____

1

TOTAL MARKS 10

Adjectives

What do adjectives do?

Adjectives are words that describe nouns. They can do lots of different things.

Adjectives are often used to describe what things or people are like.

He found a **huge green** jewel.

The **shy little** girl giggled nervously.

They can also say how many of a particular thing is being described.

I have **one** brother and **two** sisters.

Adjectives can even say who something belongs to.

He grabbed **his** bag and stormed out of **her** house.

Choosing adjectives

Adjectives are brilliant at describing what things are like, but some work much harder than others to build up a picture for your reader.

Avoid using tired, boring adjectives like *good* or *bad*. They don't say very much about the thing you are describing, because there are lots of ways that something or someone can be good or bad! Try to think about exactly what the thing is like, then choose adjectives that will give your reader that information.

The food was good.

The food was delicious.

The film was bad.

The film was boring.

Top Tip
Use a thesaurus to find better alternatives to tired or boring adjectives.

 Key words   adjective   thesaurus

Answers

PAGE 5

Planning to talk

Answers will vary, but one mark should be awarded for each piece of information.

Listening

Answers will vary, but one mark should be awarded for each point.

Questions

Answers will vary, but a mark should be awarded for writing a question.

PAGE 7

The features of books

Answers will vary.

Using the features of books

Answers will vary, but might include:

1 The blurb is a piece of information on the back of a book that gives readers an idea of what the book is about.
2 The ISBN is a unique number that is used by libraries and booksellers to identify a book.
3 The contents list lists the chapters or sections in a book.
4 The glossary is a list of technical or difficult words and their definitions.

PAGE 9

Features of fiction

Answers will vary.

Features of non-fiction

The following features may be found in a non-fiction book: charts and diagrams; lots of facts; information organised to make facts easy to find.

PAGE 11

Skimming and scanning

Skimming: 1, 4, 5
Scanning: 2, 3

Deciding what you think

Answers will vary, but might include:

1 The writer does think that the wind turbine is a good idea. They describe the school as 'forward-thinking' and write about the benefits of having a turbine.
2 Yes, because the writer says that it would make sense for other schools to install turbines and solar panels.
3 Answers will vary.

PAGE 13

What is a narrator?

1 The narrator is not likely to be a character in the story, because they are not involved in the action and are able to know that Max was late again.
2 The narrator is a character in the story, because she describes her dress and her reaction to it, so is clearly taking part in the action.

Narrator and viewpoint

Answers will vary, but might include:

1 An author might choose a narrator who is not part of the story because they can tell the reader things that none of the characters know and can see all of the characters all of the time.
2 When a character narrates the story, the reader gets to know them very well and will want to find out what happens to them.

PAGE 15

Biography

Answers will vary.

Autobiography

Answers will vary, but might include:

1 Autobiography is the story of someone's life that they write themselves.
2 The sentence that comes from an autobiography is: We travelled to Paris to meet our parents. We know this because the writer uses the words 'we' and 'our' to describe their own experiences.
3 People might be interested in reading an autobiography because it gives them an opportunity to find out about the experiences of well-known people they admire.

PAGE 17

Simple and compound sentences

1 Kate had a cold drink. She was thirsty.
2 Max found his key. He unlocked the door.
3 Jenny loves pasta. Tim likes pizza.

Complex sentences

1 <u>Mum pegged the washing on the line</u>, so it would dry.
2 <u>Amy worked hard</u>, tidying her bedroom.
3 <u>Katie ran through the rain</u>, dodging the puddles as she went.
4 <u>We left for school early</u>, so we wouldn't be late.

PAGE 19

What are contractions?

1 he's
2 she'll
3 You're
4 I'm

Using contracted forms

Yes: 1, 4, 5
No: 2, 3, 6

PAGE 21

Using possessive apostrophes

1 Our puppy's toys are in its basket.
2 The twins' desks are side by side.
3 The sun's rays shone through the window.
4 Two ponies' saddles hung on the wall.
5 Jacob's dad is a fireman.

Its and it's

1 The gate squeaks when **it's** opened.
2 The dog chased **its** tail.
3 Mum put the key back on **its** hook.
4 **It's** too cold to swim in the sea.
5 The horse shook **its** mane.

PAGE 23

Commas

1 When we got hungry, we ate our picnic.
2 Last summer, we went to Spain.
3 Billy went to bed, yawning loudly.
4 Eventually, the sun came out.
5 The dog ran after the postman, barking as he went.

Colons and semi-colons

1 We took a picnic; it was a lovely day.
2 I love Chinese food; Max prefers Italian meals.
3 I found my umbrella; it was starting to rain.
4 The sea was rough; we could not swim.
5 The doorbell rang; my friends had arrived.

PAGE 25

Direct and reported speech

Answers may vary.

1 The bus driver explained, "There are empty seats at the back of the bus."
2 "Get ready for assembly," said Mrs Drew.
3 "Please could I have a strawberry milkshake?" asked Ben.
4 "The present is hidden under my bed," whispered Daisy.
5 "I'm sorry I spilt my drink," apologised Ryan.

Introducing direct speech

1 "Don't worry, we can mend it," **comforted** Mum.
2 "You must clean up your room," **insisted** Dad.
3 "Don't forget your homework," **reminded** the teacher.
4 "When is your birthday?" **asked** Beth.
5 "Hurray!" **cheered** the class.

PAGE 27

Common nouns

Answers may vary.

1 cinema
2 car
3 book

Proper nouns

1 Last <u>wednesday</u> was <u>christopher's</u> birthday.
2 We are going to <u>france</u> on holiday this <u>august</u>.
3 The <u>nile</u> flows through <u>egypt</u>.

Pronouns

1 We hid from my brother so he wouldn't see <u>us</u>.
2 The wind rocked the tree until <u>it</u> was blown over.
3 Ben's shoes were dirty, so <u>he</u> cleaned <u>them</u>.
4 Debbie's hamster escaped but <u>she</u> caught <u>it</u>.

PAGE 29

Simple plurals

1 foxes
2 dishes
3 plants
4 bosses
5 watches

Words ending in y

1 keys
2 puppies
3 plays
4 fairies

Words ending in f

Answers may vary.

With most words that end in f, you have to change the f to ves to make the plural. There are a few exceptions e.g. roofs.

PAGE 31

What do adjectives do?

1 small, thick
2 five, one
3 his, my

Choosing adjectives

1   huge, enormous, gigantic
2   ancient, elderly, aged
3   naughty, evil, mischievous
4   starving, peckish, ravenous

PAGE 33

Choosing verbs

1   The hungry boy <u>gobbled</u> the fruit.
2   The man <u>sprinted</u> to catch his train.
3   The squirrel <u>scampered</u> up the tree.
4   The cat <u>howled</u> on the fence.
5   The fire <u>crackled</u> in the grate.

Verb tenses

Add *ed*: enjoyed, wished
Add *d*: glared, smiled
Double the final letter and add *ed*: trimmed

Irregular verb endings

1   Mum <u>hided</u> my Christmas presents, but I found them anyway.
2   My brother had chicken pox and then I <u>catched</u> it.
3   We <u>goed</u> shopping for new shoes.
4   Mum <u>humed</u> a tune as she washed the car.
5   I <u>writed</u> a brilliant story but I lost it on the way home.

PAGE 35

How adverbs work

Answers will vary, but might include:
1   The hamster spun **quickly** in its wheel.
2   Autumn leaves drifted **gently** from the trees.
3   The class listened **carefully** to the teacher.
4   The sun shone **brightly** all day.
5   Ballerinas danced **gracefully** across the stage.

Making adverbs

The following adjectives can be turned into adverbs by adding *ly*:
brave, cheerful, careless, quiet, fresh, sad, beautiful, bold

PAGE 37

Finding synonyms

Answers will vary, but might include:
1   journey
2   present
3   cup
4   consume
5   sea
6   doze

Using synonyms

Answers will vary, but might include:
1   We opened the **hen** house to feed the chickens.
2   They found a little village and **discovered** a bakery that sold delicious cakes.
3   The little **stream** flowed past the village green, then joined a bigger river.
4   Our new **home** is bigger than our old house.

PAGE 39

Simile, metaphor and personification

1   Skaters glided past like swans.
2   The ice was a sheet of glass.
3   …their skates whispering to each other.

Using imagery

1   Hundreds of birds chattered in the trees. This is personification.
2   The sea churned like a washing machine. This is simile.
3   The river was a ribbon on the landscape. This is metaphor.

PAGE 41

Alliteration and onomatopoeia

Answers will vary, but might include:
1   The flag flapped and fluttered in the breeze.
2   The twig snapped beneath my shoe, startling the deer.

Reading special effects

1   glossy and golden. Gorgeous! – Draws attention to how good the egg yolk looks.
2   sauce squelched on soft slices – Draws attention to the softness and freshness of the bread.
3   sizzle – Draws attention to the sound of the egg frying.
4   squelched – Draws attention to the sound the sauce makes.

PAGE 43

The imperative

1   Make sure that both surfaces are clean and dry.
2   Spread the glue in a thin, even layer on both surfaces.
3   Allow the glue to dry slightly before joining the surfaces.

Organising instructions

1   Write your letter.
2   Put the letter in an envelope.
3   Write an address on the envelope.
4   Post the letter.

PAGE 45

Writing persuasive text

Answers will vary, but might include:

1 The hotel boasts a huge swimming pool with many amazing slides.
2 Glitz will wash your clothes brilliantly and has a fantastic fresh smell.
3 Megascreen cinemas screen all the latest blockbusters.

Setting out persuasive writing

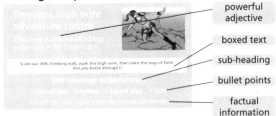

- powerful adjective
- boxed text
- sub-heading
- bullet points
- factual information

PAGE 47

Features of recounts

When we arrived at the cinema, the lights were on and the curtains were closed. **Suddenly** the lights dimmed and the curtains opened. **Next** some adverts came on, showing films that would be released soon. **During** those, we got comfortable and shared round the popcorn. **Eventually** the film began.

Planning recounts

Answers will vary.

PAGE 49

Features of reports

Reports are **non-fiction** texts. They are not written **chronologically**. Instead, the information is arranged in **topics**. Reports are often written in the **present** tense. They are normally written using quite **formal** language.

Report language

The continent of Africa <u>is a giant</u>. It includes 53 countries, in which more than 100 languages are spoken. The Nile is the longest river in the world, <u>striding</u> through Uganda, Sudan and Egypt. <u>Africa's</u> home to 800 million people, as

well as four of the world's five fastest animals, including the cheetah. <u>It's</u> <u>as quick as a flash</u>, running at 70 miles per hour.

PAGE 51

Planning a story

events	4
opening	1
dilemma	3
build-up	2
resolution	5

Openings

Answers will vary.

Endings

Answers will vary.

PAGE 53

Developing characters

Answers will vary.

Describing settings

Answers will vary, but one mark should be awarded for each phrase.

PAGE 55

List poems

Answers will vary, but might include:

Hot is… the summer sun,

Steaming cocoa,

Spicy curry,

Hearty soups,

Log fires in winter.

Kennings poems

Answers will vary, but might include:

Puddle-maker,

Umbrella-beater,

Flood-bringer,

Street-washer,

Plant-grower.

Letts Educational
4 Grosvenor Place, London SW1X 7DL
Orders: 015395 64910
Enquiries: 015395 65921
Email: enquiries@lettsandlonsdale.co.uk
Website: www.lettsandlonsdale.com

First published 2009

Editorial and design: 2ibooks [publishing solutions] Cambridge

Author: Alison Head
Book concept and development: Helen Jacobs, Publishing Director
Editorial: Sophie London, Senior Commissioning Editor
　　　　Katy Knight, Junior Editor
Illustrators: Andy Roberts and Phillip Burrows
Cover design: Angela English

British Library Cataloging in Publication Data. A CIP record of this book is available from the British Library.

ISBN 9781844192151

Text, design and illustration © 2008 Letts Educational Ltd

Printed in Dubai

Letts Educational make every effort to ensure that all paper used in our books made from wood pulp obtained from well-managed forests, controlled source and recycled wood or fibre.

What do adjectives do?

Read this piece of text, then answer the questions.

> Five letters arrived that day. One small brown one was a bill for Dad. The bank statement was his, too. My letter was a thick white envelope. I couldn't wait to see what was inside.

1 Find and copy two adjectives that describe the size of something.

_____

2 Find and copy two adjectives that describe the quantity of something.

_____

3 Find and copy two adjectives that describe who something belongs to.

_____

3

Choosing adjectives

Write down three adjectives from the box which could be used instead of each of the tired adjectives.

starving   naughty   ancient   evil   peckish   huge

mischievous   enormous   ravenous   elderly   gigantic   aged

1 big

_____

2 old

_____

3 bad

_____

4 hungry

_____

12

TOTAL MARKS 15

Verbs

Choosing verbs

Verbs describe what people and things in our sentences are doing. Choosing verbs carefully helps you to build up a vivid picture of what is happening for your reader.

> The baby **toddled** outside. The baby **walked** outside.

Toddled is a better verb to describe how a baby walks.

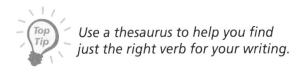 *Use a thesaurus to help you find just the right verb for your writing.*

Verb tenses

Verbs can tell us when something happened by changing their tense.

> I worked hard yesterday. (past tense)
>
> I am working hard today. (present tense)
>
> I shall work hard tomorrow. (future tense)

Lots of past tense verbs end in *ed*.

wash ➜ washed

If the verb already ends in *e*, you just add *d*.

move ➜ moved

Other times, you have to double the final letter first.

plan ➜ planned

Irregular verb endings

Lots of past tense verbs do not end in *ed*. Instead, they change completely in the past tense.

> catch ➜ caught   see ➜ saw   go ➜ went

Some of the verbs that we use most often have an irregular past tense. It is worth learning them so you can use them properly in your writing.

Key words   tense   past tense   present tense   future tense

Choosing verbs

Underline the best verb in each pair to complete each sentence.

1   The hungry boy (gobbled nibbled) the fruit.

2   The man (ambled sprinted) to catch his train.

3   The squirrel (scampered jogged) up the tree.

4   The cat (yelled howled) on the fence.

5   The fire (crunched crackled) in the grate.

5

Verb tenses

Write down the past tense of these verbs in the correct box.

enjoy   glare   wish   trim   smile

add *ed*	add *d*	double the final letter and add *ed*

5

Irregular verb endings

Underline the incorrect past tense verbs in these sentences.

1   Mum hided my Christmas presents, but I found them anyway.

2   My brother had chicken pox and then I catched it.

3   We goed shopping for new shoes.

4   Mum humed a tune as she washed the car.

5   I writed a brilliant story but I lost it on the way home.

5

TOTAL MARKS   15

Adverbs

How adverbs work

Adverbs are words that describe verbs. They work by adding information about how an action takes place.

Every sentence contains a verb, but not all verbs say enough about the action. Choosing the right adverb will help to improve your writing by creating a picture in your reader's mind.

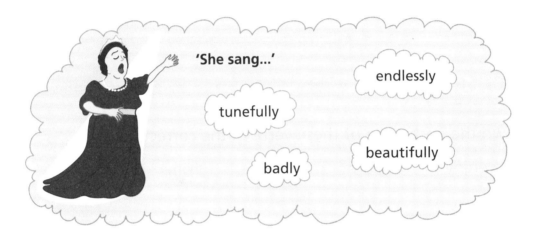

Think carefully about the picture you are trying to create when you choose your adverb.

Making adverbs

Many adverbs end in *ly* and you can sometimes make an adverb by adding *ly* to an adjective.

clever + ly = cleverly

bold + ly = boldly

sad + ly = sadly

rapid + ly = rapidly

huge + ly = hugely

Top Tip *Don't forget the spelling rule for adding **ly** to words ending in **y**, e.g. happy + ly = happily.*

Key words   adverb

How adverbs work

Think of a suitable adverb to fill the gap in each sentence.

1 The hamster spun _____ in its wheel.

2 Autumn leaves drifted _____ from the trees.

3 The class listened _____ to the teacher.

4 The sun shone _____ all day.

5 Ballerinas danced _____ across the stage.

5

Making adverbs

Circle the adjectives that can be turned into adverbs by adding *ly*.

blue   quiet

brave

bold

careless

sad

fresh

cheerful

small   big

old

beautiful   posh

8

TOTAL MARKS 13

35

Synonyms

Finding synonyms

Synonyms are words with similar meanings. Nouns, verbs, adverbs and adjectives can all have synonyms and some words have several.

sleep ➜ doze ➜ slumber

rain ➜ drizzle ➜ sleet

sweets ➜ candies ➜ confectionery

Many of the words we use a lot have synonyms. They can help you to avoid using the same word again and again in your writing.

Using synonyms

If you keep using the same word again and again in your writing, it will be very boring to read. Instead, look for words with similar meanings to add a bit of variety.

We crossed the main **road** and walked down a little **road** towards the beach.

We crossed the main **road** and walked down a little **lane** towards the beach.

Dad **built** a path to the shed he had **built**.

Dad **constructed** a path to the shed he had **built**.

Read your writing through when you have finished and think about whether you need to swap any words for their synonyms, in order to avoid repetition and add variety.

Top Tip *Synonyms have similar meanings, but very few mean exactly the same thing. Take care to choose the best one for each sentence.*

Key words | synonym

Finding synonyms

Think of a synonym for each of these common words.

1 trip _____ 4 eat _____

2 gift _____ 5 ocean _____

3 mug _____ 6 sleep _____

6

Using synonyms

Write these sentences again, using synonyms to avoid repetition.

1 We opened the chicken house to feed the chickens.

_____

_____

2 They found a little village and found a bakery that sold delicious cakes.

_____

_____

3 The little river flowed past the village green, then joined a bigger river.

_____

_____

4 Our new house is bigger than our old house.

_____

_____

_____

4

TOTAL MARKS 10

Imagery

Simile, metaphor and personification

Simile, metaphor and personification are all types of imagery that you can use to create vivid descriptions in your writing.

Similes compare two things using the words *as* or *like*.

> My cakes came out of the oven as hard as rocks.

Metaphors describe a thing as if it really were something else.

> The lightning was a silver fork across the sky.

Personification is another type of imagery, where non-human things are described using human characteristics.

> The stars winked cheerfully in the night sky.

If you are asked to write about a piece of writing that someone else has done, be ready to write about the imagery the author has used.

Top Tip *Imagery tends not to be used in non-fiction writing like formal letters, instructions, recounts or reports.*

Using imagery

When you are choosing imagery to use in your writing, think about the effect you are trying to achieve.

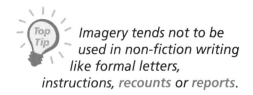

> The curry was a fire in my mouth.

Imagine what a really spicy curry tastes like.
Describing the taste as a fire helps the reader to understand how hot it is.

If you can't think of your own imagery, try using a more well-known simile or metaphor. Try to avoid the really common ones though, as they can sound boring.

 Key words   simile   metaphor   personification   imagery   recount   report

Simile, metaphor and personification

Read this piece of text and answer the questions.

The ice was a sheet of glass. Skaters glided past like swans, carving patterns in the ice with their sharp skates. Couples skated arm in arm in wide circles, their skates whispering to each other.

1   Find and copy an example of simile.

_____

2   Find and copy an example of metaphor.

_____

3   Find and copy an example of personification.

_____

Top Tip   *Reading tests may ask you to state why you think a writer has used a particular word. Be ready to talk about any imagery they have used.*

3

Using imagery

Match up each of these things with the more effective way to describe it. Then write whether simile, metaphor or personification has been used.

1   Hundreds of birds

1 discussed in the trees.

2 chattered in the trees.

_____

2   The sea churned

3 like a washing machine.

4 as quick as a flash.

_____

3   The river was

5 a string on the landscape.

6 a ribbon on the landscape.

_____

3

TOTAL MARKS   6

39

Special effects

Alliteration and onomatopoeia

The way words sound can help you to create brilliant effects in your writing.

Alliteration is where words that start with the same sound are used together. When they are read out, the repeated sound helps to draw your reader's attention to that part of the writing.

Losing her balance, she **s**lipped and **s**lid on the **s**oft **s**now.

Onomatopoeia is where words sound like the things they describe.

Sarah **slurped** her drink.

The snake **slithered** quickly away through the grass.

Onomatopoeia works well because with just one word your reader will be able to imagine exactly how something sounds.

*Remember, it is the sound and not the letter that is important in alliteration, so **phantom** would go with **followed** rather than **played**.*

Reading special effects

Being able to spot techniques like alliteration and onomatopoeia in other people's writing will get you extra marks in reading tests. Writers put them there on purpose, so always make a note of where they have been used and which bits of the text they are designed to draw your attention to.

Mist rolled in rapidly, wrapping the town in gloom. Streetlights came on early and motorists turned on their headlights. Somewhere in the fog, a car alarm wailed.

Alliteration describes the weather.   Onomatopoeia describes the sound of the car.

 Key words   alliteration   onomatopoeia

Alliteration and onomatopoeia

1 Write this sentence again, using alliteration to draw the reader's attention to how the flag is moving.

The flag blew and waved in the breeze.

_____

2 Write this sentence again, using onomatopoeia to draw the reader's attention to the sound of the twig breaking.

The twig broke beneath my shoe, startling the deer.

_____

2

Reading special effects

I broke an egg into the pan and let it sizzle. The yolk was glossy and golden. Gorgeous! Tomato sauce squelched on soft slices of bread, ready for the fried egg. My mouth watered.

Find and copy two examples of alliteration, then write what each example is designed to draw your attention to.

1 Example 1

_____

3 Example 2

_____

2 what it draws your attention to

_____

4 what it draws your attention to

_____

Find and copy two examples of onomatopoeia, then write what each example is designed to draw your attention to.

5 Example 3

_____

7 Example 4

_____

6 what it draws your attention to

_____

8 what it draws your attention to

_____

8

Instructions

The imperative

There are lots of different types of instructions. Recipes, road signs and directions on how to make something or get to a place are all types of instructions. You will also find instructions on packaged foods, medicines and toiletries.

Instructions do not ask you to do something; they tell you!

They do this using something called the imperative. This means using the verb first, without a noun or pronoun before it.

Preheat the oven to 200°C.

Place the pizza directly on the oven shelf.

Bake for 12 minutes or until the cheese is bubbling.

Organising instructions

Instructions break a task down into small steps, which are sometimes written as bullet points or numbered lists.

Longer or more complicated steps sometimes use connective words or phrases to show when to do each thing.

1 Place the margarine in a pan over a low heat **until** it has melted.

2 Add the sugar **and** stir **while** it dissolves.

3 Remove the mixture from the heat **before** it boils.

However they are written, the tasks must always be described in the correct order, or the user may end up with an unexpected result! They are often numbered to make sure they are followed in the right order.

Top Tip If you are asked to write some instructions, think in detail about how you would complete the task, so that you don't miss out any important steps.

 Key words | imperative

The imperative

Write these sentences again, using the imperative to turn them into instructions.

1 You need to make sure that both surfaces are clean and dry.

_____

2 You should spread the glue in a thin, even layer on both surfaces.

_____

3 The glue should be allowed to dry slightly before joining the surfaces.

_____

3

Organising instructions

Number these instructions 1–4 to put them in the correct order, then write in the missing step.

☐ _____

☐ Post the letter.

☐ Put the letter in an envelope.

☐ Write your letter.

 Top Tip _Try using a flow chart to help you to arrange the steps in the right order._

4

TOTAL MARKS 7

Persuasive writing

Writing persuasive text

Persuasive writing, like adverts and brochures, aims to convince the reader to adopt a particular point of view, or to buy a product or visit an attraction.

Most persuasive writing uses very few words, to make it quick and easy for people to read. Every word has to work hard to persuade the reader, so use really powerful adjectives and think carefully about how you can build up a convincing argument. Don't just say that the product you are writing about is the best. You need to say **why** it is the best. Focus on the benefits the reader will get if they choose your product or idea.

> The book provides a *fascinating* insight into the *glamorous* world of the rich and famous.
>
> You can get closer than ever before to your favourite stars!

 Top Tip *If you are asked to do some persuasive writing, think about what would make you choose that product or idea, then base your argument on that.*

Setting out persuasive writing

Collect some leaflets, posters and brochures and have a look at how they set out the writing.

Persuasive writing is not always set out in complete sentences. Instead, it may use bullet points, text in boxes and sub-headings to organise the information. Key information may be underlined, or presented bold, or in a different colour.

It may need to include facts as well as persuasion. Posters and leaflets often include information like addresses and opening times, as well as prices and special offers.

 Key words   persuasive writing

Writing persuasive text

Write these dull sentences again, using powerful descriptions to persuade the reader.

1 The hotel has a very big swimming pool with lots of slides.

_____

2 Glitz will wash your clothes very well and has a nice smell.

_____

3 Megascreen cinemas show all the new films.

_____

3

Setting out persuasive writing

Read this piece of persuasive writing, then draw lines to join each of the features listed to an example within the text.

1 sub-heading   **2** bullet points   **3** factual information

4 powerful adjective   **5** boxed text

Treetops high wire adventure centre
The new extreme climbing experience for over-10s!

Scale our 30ft climbing wall, walk the high wire, then take the leap of faith.
Are you brave enough?!

The treetops experience...
• **Helmet hire** • **Parties** • **School trips** • **Café**
Just off the A40. Open every day except Christmas.

5

Recounts

Features of recounts

Recounts tell the reader about something that has happened. It could be about a school trip, someone's life, a historical event or something funny that has happened to you.

Recounts are always written in the past tense and the events are described in the order in which they happened. They are often linked together with time connectives like *first*, *next* and *after that*, which help to make the order of events clearer.

Because recounts are non-fiction, they don't tend to contain imagery like simile, metaphor and personification.

Planning recounts

Recounts are quite easy to plan and write, because you can just write about each event one at a time, in chronological order.

You can plan your recount using a time line or flow chart, which are quick ways to jot down the key events. They will both help you to put events in the correct order and ensure that you do not leave anything out.

Time line

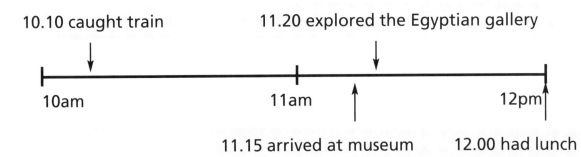

10.10 caught train   11.20 explored the Egyptian gallery

10am   11am   12pm

11.15 arrived at museum   12.00 had lunch

Once you have organised the events, you can write a short paragraph on each event, linked together with suitable time connectives.

Time lines and flow charts are great for organising your ideas in tests, but don't spend too long on them, as they won't be marked.

Key words   time connective

Features of recounts

Pick suitable time connectives from the box to complete this recount.

Next   When   During   Eventually   Suddenly

_____ we arrived at the cinema, the lights were on and the curtains were closed. _____ the lights dimmed and the curtains opened. _____ some adverts came on, showing films that would be released soon. _____ those, we got comfortable and shared round the popcorn. _____ the film began.

5

Planning recounts

Draw a flow chart or time line, showing **five** of the main things that happened to you between leaving home and arriving at school.

5

TOTAL MARKS   10

Reports

Features of reports

A report is a piece of factual writing about a particular subject. Reports can be about almost any topic, so you will probably have to write them in other classes, as well as English.

The information in reports is organised into topics, rather than chronologically. If you are asked to write a report, you will need to decide on a logical way to organise your ideas. Research your topic first, then decide which pieces of information you want to include. Finally, use a spidergram or tree diagram to group your ideas together.

Once you have a plan, you can simply write a paragraph for each section of your plan.

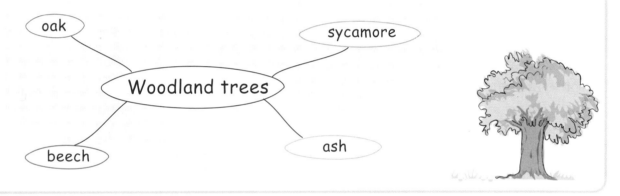

Report language

Reports are often written in the present tense, unless they are about a historical period.

They are non-fiction, so you would not usually use imagery like simile, metaphor and personification. Instead, the language used tends to be quite formal and you might also need to use technical vocabulary that goes with the subject. For example, if you were writing a report about renewable energy, you would need to use terms like *solar panel* and *wind turbine*.

Top Tip

*Don't use contractions like **don't** or **isn't** in reports, because they need to be written more formally, i.e. **do not** or **is not**.*

Key words   spidergram

Features of reports

Choose words from the box to complete this piece of writing about reports.

fiction   non-fiction   chronologically   topics
present   past   future   formal   informal

Reports are _____ texts. They are not written

_____. Instead, the information is arranged in

_____. Reports are often written in the

_____ tense. They are normally written using

quite _____ language.

5

Report language

Read the report, then underline **five** words or phrases you would not normally expect to see in a report.

The continent of Africa is a giant. It includes 53 countries, in which more than 100 languages are spoken. The Nile is the longest river in the world, striding through Uganda, Sudan and Egypt. Africa's home to 800 million people, as well as four of the world's five fastest animals, including the cheetah. It's as quick as a flash, running at 70 miles per hour.

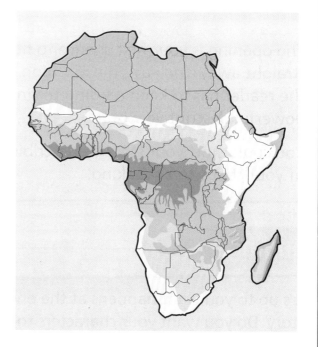

5

TOTAL MARKS   10

Planning stories

Planning a story

Planning a story will save you time in a test by helping you to get your ideas in order before you start to write. Try thinking about the story in five sections.

1 Opening: introduces the characters and settings.

2 Build-up: allows the events running up to the big dilemma to unfold.

3 Dilemma: explains the problems the characters have to overcome.

4 Events: tell how the characters try to overcome the problems.

5 Resolution: explains how the characters resolve the problems posed in the story.

Openings

The opening is your first chance to hook your reader, so start the action straight away. Try leaving a question hanging in the first few sentences, so the reader has to keep reading to find out what happens next. Use lots of powerful descriptive words.

You could start your story by describing a character or setting, or with one of your characters speaking.

Endings

It's up to you what happens at the end of your story. Do you want your characters to be happy or to learn a lesson about their behaviour? Make sure the ending follows on properly from the story, without seeming 'tacked on' to the end.

Top Tip *Try to leave your reader with something to think about after the story has finished.*

Planning a story

Add the missing names to each of the sections of this story plan. Then number them 1–5 to put them in the correct order.

Explains how the characters try to overcome their difficulties.   _____ ☐

Describes the characters and settings.   _____ ☐

Explains the difficulties faced by the characters.   _____ ☐

Explains how events unfold running up to the big dilemma.   _____ ☐

Shows how the characters eventually overcome the problems they face.   _____ ☐

5

Openings

Think about the well-known fairy tale *Jack and the Beanstalk*. It starts with Jack trading the family's cow for some magic beans. Write a new opening for the story, giving the tale a modern setting.

_____

_____

1

Endings

In the fairy tale, Jack's mother cuts down the beanstalk after Jack has climbed down with the treasure, so that the giant can't follow. Jot down some notes about an alternative ending for the story.

_____

_____

1

TOTAL MARKS ⬭ 7

Developing characters

Characters are the most important part of a story. If they are interesting and believable, people will want to read on in order to find out what happens to them.

Avoid flat, boring characters by thinking carefully about what each character would behave, sound and look like if they were real. Spend time developing characters before you start writing, so they seem real right from the start.

Think about the role that each character will play in the plot and try to match it with their personality. So if a character will be a hero or heroine in the story, make them seem brave right from the start.

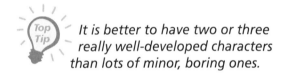

Top Tip *It is better to have two or three really well-developed characters than lots of minor, boring ones.*

Describing settings

The setting is the place where the story happens, but it should be more than just a backdrop. Use imagery like simile, metaphor and personification to help your readers to imagine what your settings look, sound, smell and feel like. If you are writing a science fiction story, try creating a space-age setting. For a ghost story, describe a spooky haunted house.

Developing characters

Characters don't have to be nice to be interesting. Villains can be great, because people want to find out if something unpleasant happens to them! Write a character profile for a really mean teacher in a story about an old-fashioned boarding school.

1 Name: _____

2 Age: _____

3 Personality: ☐ cruel   ☐ sarcastic

☐ funny   ☐ dishonest

4 Descriptive words to describe how he/she looks:

_____

5 How does he/she feel about the children at the school?

_____

6 How might this character contribute to the story's plot?

_____

6

Describing settings

Now think about a classroom setting you could use for the story. Write four creative phrases you could use to describe it.

1 _____

2 _____

3 _____

4 _____

4

WRITING

53

Poetry

LEARN

WRITING

List poems

Writing poems can be a bit daunting, but there are lots of simple poetry styles that allow you to show off your best creative writing techniques.

A **list poem** is just a list of powerful descriptions, based on the same subject. List poems do not need to rhyme and because each description is self-contained, you can use a different technique for each one. Try using creative techniques like simile, metaphor, personification, alliteration or onomatopoeia.

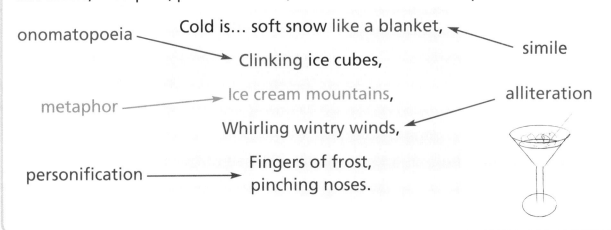

onomatopoeia

Cold is… soft snow like a blanket,

Clinking ice cubes,

simile

metaphor

Ice cream mountains,

alliteration

Whirling wintry winds,

personification

Fingers of frost, pinching noses.

Kennings poems

A **kenning** is a way of describing something without saying what it is. You can join up several kennings to make a poem. The reader has to play detective to work out what the poem is about and each kenning acts as a clue. Make sure you pick some powerful descriptive sentences to create a picture for the reader.

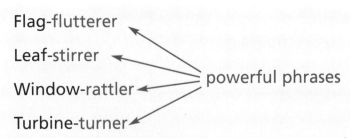

Flag-flutterer

Leaf-stirrer

Window-rattler

Turbine-turner

powerful phrases

Did you work out that the poem was about the wind?

Key words   list poem   kenning

List poems

Complete this list poem by adding five descriptions to the list.

Hot is… _____

_____

_____

_____

_____

5

Kennings poems

Write a five-line kennings poem about the rain.

_____

_____

_____

_____

_____

 Top Tip *Rhythm is important in most poems. Try reading your poem aloud to see if it sounds right.*

5

TOTAL MARKS 10

Glossary

GLOSSARY

adjective a word or phrase that describes a noun

adverb a word or phrase that describes a verb

alliteration a phrase where most or all of the words begin with the same sound

apostrophe a punctuation mark used for contraction, when two words are joined, or to show possession, e.g. We'll collect Dad's car.

author the person who writes a text

autobiography the story of someone's life that they write themselves

biography the story of someone's life written by someone else

blurb information on the back of a book designed to give the reader an idea of what it is about

clause a distinct part of a sentence including a verb

colon a punctuation mark that can be used to introduce explanations or lists

comma a punctuation mark that shows when to pause, separates clauses, or separates items in a list

common noun a noun that names ordinary things, e.g. book, car

complex sentence a sentence that contains a main clause and a subordinate clause

compound sentence a sentence that contains two equally weighted clauses, joined together with a conjunction

comprehension understanding what a text is about

conjunction a word used to link sentences or clauses, or to connect words within a phrase, e.g. so, and, later

consonant any letter of the alphabet except the vowels a, e, i, o and u

contraction when words are shortened, or two words are joined, by removing letters and replacing with an apostrophe, e.g. can't, won't

dialogue a spoken or written conversation between two people

direct speech words that are actually spoken, enclosed in speech marks

fiction stories with imaginary characters, settings or events

first person events told in the first person are told from the viewpoint of the person doing an action, e.g. I am playing chess.

future tense describes things that will happen in the future

glossary a collection of useful words and their meanings

imagery words used to build up a picture in a story, including simile, metaphor and personification

imperative a way of using verbs to give an order or instruction, e.g. Turn left at the traffic lights.

index an alphabetical list of the topics in a book

ISBN a unique number on the back of a book used by booksellers and libraries

kenning a way of describing a thing without naming it

list poem a poem made up of a list of descriptions of the same thing

main clause the main part of a sentence which makes sense on its own

metaphor where a writer describes something as if it were something else, e.g. The bird was an arrow, tearing across the sky.

narrator the person from whose viewpoint a story is told. May or may not be a character in the story

non-fiction writing that is not fictional, including information texts about real people and places, letters, instructions and reports

noun a word that names a thing or feeling

onomatopoeia when a word sounds like the noise it describes, e.g. crash, shatter

opinion what someone thinks or believes

past tense describes things that have already happened

personification a writing technique in which human characteristics are used to describe non-human things, e.g. Shadows crept across the floor.

persuasive writing writing that aims to persuade the reader to adopt a particular point of view, e.g. newspaper adverts

plural more than one of something, usually made by adding s or es, e.g. dogs, dresses

possessive apostrophe an apostrophe used to show that something belongs to someone, e.g. Sarah's homework

present tense describes things that are happening now

pronoun a word used instead of a noun to avoid having to use the same noun again, e.g. I, she, we, me

proper noun a noun that names a specific person, thing or place, e.g. Chris, Manchester, Friday

recount a report that describes events in chronological order, or the order in which they happened

report an information text about a particular subject

reported speech speech reported in a text, but not directly quoted, e.g. She said she was tired.

scanning reading quickly to find a specific piece of information

semi-colon a punctuation mark used to join clauses in a sentence where one adds information to the other

sentence a unit of text that makes sense on its own

simile where a writer compares one thing with another, using the words as or like, e.g. as bold as brass

simple sentence a sentence containing one clause

singular one of something, e.g. a bird

skimming reading quickly to understand the main meaning of a piece of text

speech marks punctuation marks that surround direct speech. Other punctuation goes inside them, e.g. "Goodbye," said Mum.

spidergram a diagram that helps writers to organise their ideas around a particular theme

subject the person or thing in a sentence that carries out the action, e.g. Amy bit the apple.

subordinate clause a clause which adds extra information to the main clause, but does not make sense on its own

synonym a word with exactly or nearly the same meaning as another word, e.g. hot, warm

tense tells us when something is happening

thesaurus a book of synonyms

third person events told in the third person are told from the viewpoint of someone other than the person doing an action, e.g. She is working hard today.

time connective a word or phrase that helps to explain when something happened, e.g. first, after that, finally

verb a doing or being word, e.g. walk, sleep

viewpoint how a story is told from a specific character's way of looking at things

vowel a, e, i, o and u. The other letters in the alphabet are consonants